What's a ghost's favorite dinner?
Spookhetti

• • •

What's the speed limit in Egypt?
60 Niles an hour

• • •

What stopped the two elephants from going for a swim on a hot day?
They only had one pair of trunks between them.

• • •

What's covered in feathers and cracks jokes?
A comedi-hen

1,000 WHAT'S WHAT JOKES FOR KIDS

by Michael Johnstone

BALLANTINE BOOKS • NEW YORK

ISBN 0-345-34654-8

This edition published by arrangement with Ward Lock Ltd.

Manufactured in the United States of America

First Ballantine Books Edition: December 1987
Second Printing: April 1988

Contents

What?

What's red and goes "Ho, ho, plop"?
Santa Claus laughing his head off

What's black and white and flies?
Supernun

What's green and camps?
A Boy Sprout

What's best for sick birds?
  Tweatment

What's the national anthem of the jungle?
  "Tarzan Stripes Forever"

What's got six legs and can't walk?
  Three pairs of pants

What's served and never eaten?
  A tennis ball

What's sweet and swings from tree to tree?
  Tarzipan

What's Tarzan's favorite carol?
  "Jungle Bells"

What's 300 yards tall, weighs 7,620 tons and attracts bees?
  The Eiffel Flower

What made the Boy Scout dizzy?
  Too many good turns

What's hot and moves at 100 miles an hour?
A man running a temperature

What's got two legs and bursts into flames?
Flared pants

What does a thief's son do?
He takes after his father

What's the trampolinist's motto?
"Life has its ups and downs, but you can always bounce back."

What's black, lives in Scotland, and knew Eve?
   Tarmacadam

What's wrapped in silver foil and has an on/off switch?
   A TV dinner

What's chocolate outside, peanut inside, and sings hymns?
   A Sunday School Tweet

What's the best way to make trousers last?
   Wear the jacket first

What's the time when the clock strikes thirteen?
  Time to get a new clock

What's green, has two legs and a trunk?
  A seasick vacationer

What's good for keeping a person from sleepwalking?
  Tacks on the floor

What's white on the outside, pink in the middle, and talks to itself?
  A tongue sandwich

What's the better fighter—a turnip or a chicken?
   A turnip—it's no chicken.

What's a twitch?
   A nervous witch

What's a waiter's favorite sport?
   Tennis—it improves his service.

What's red, round, and cheeky?
   Tomato sauce

What's brown and sneaks around the kitchen at Thanksgiving?
    Mince spies

What's gray and white and runs from New York to L.A. without moving?
    The interstate

What's Santa Claus's wife called?
    Mary Christmas

What's the best way to stop milk from going sour?
    Drink it when it's fresh.

What's yellow and smells of bananas?
    A monkey that's been sick

What's got two legs, two arms, and is good on a dark night?
    A light-headed man

What's big, bright, and silly?
    A fool moon

What's good at adding and subtracting, and bumps into flames?
    A mothematician

What's John McEnroe's least favorite film?
   The Umpire Strikes Back

What's the best thing to do with a blue monster?
   Cheer him up.

What's the best thing to do with a green monster?
   Wait until he's ripe.

What's woolly, covered in chocolate, and floats around the sun?
   A Mars baa

What's soft, sweet, white, and comes from Mars?
    A martianmallow

What's got forty-eight heads and no tails?
    A box of matches

What's gray, has whiskers, and squeaks?
    A mouse on roller skates

What's the best way to raise money?
    Lift it with a spoon.

What did Noah use to see in the dark?
  Floodlights

What's black and white and has four wheels?
  A nun on a skateboard

What's the best thing to do if your nose goes on strike?
  Pick-it.

What's four and five, if two's company and three's a crowd?
  Nine

What's awarded to designers of door-knockers?
   The No-bell prize

What happened when a truckload of hair restorer was spilled on the highway?
   Police combed the area.

What happened when ten beds were stolen from a warehouse?
   The police sprang into action.

What happened when someone drilled a hole in the nudist colony fence?
   The police looked into it.

What's bright red and thick?
    A blood clot

What's black and white, black and white, black and white, black and white?
    A nun falling downstairs

What's black and white and comes out of the oven spitting mad?
    A hot cross nun

What's black and white and goes up and down twenty times a day?
    A nun doing push-ups

What's brown and causes panic in a convent?
    A raised toilet seat

What are long, pointed, and run in families?
    Noses

What's red and runs at 100 miles an hour?
    The Bionic Nose

What's a dead man's nose called?
    The dead scenter

What's an operator?
  Someone who can't stand opera

What's black, white, and red?
  A newspaper

What's black, hairy, and surrounded by water?
  An oil wig

What's the dirtiest part of a ship?
  The officers' mess

What's round, white, and giggles?
  A tickled onion

16

What's round, white, and jumps around the garden?
  A spring onion

What's copper nitrate?
  A policeman's overtime

What's doughy and 50 yards high?
  The Leaning Tower of Pizza

What relation is a doorstep to a doormat?
  Stepfarther

What do you get if you dial 666?
  Australian policemen

What's yellow and white and travels at 2,000 miles an hour?
   A Concorde pilot's egg sandwich

What's the speed limit in Egypt?
   60 Niles an hour

What's blue and white and full of fuzz?
   A police car

What's a polygon?
   A dead parrot

What's white, round, and smells?
  A ping-ponging ball

What's a policeman with twenty children called?
  "Daddy"

What's the best present for a man with everything?
  Penicillin

What's red, spreads, and shouldn't be broken?
  A rash promise

What's politics?
   A parrot that's swallowed an alarm clock

What's gray, lumpy, and comes at you from four sides?
   Quadraphonic porridge

What's red and white and full of policemen?
   A sunburned panda

What's yellow, furry, and rides along the seashore?
   A peach buggy

What's a carpenter's favorite TV show?
   "Plankety plank"

What makes a piano laugh?
   Someone tickling the ivories

What made the projector blush?
   It saw the film strip.

What's yellow and fills fields with music?
   Popcorn

What's an inkling?
   A baby fountain pen

What's the Pope's airplane called?
   The Holy-copter

What's feathered, clucks, and wins Wimbledon?
Boris Pecker

What's the most popular gardening magazine in the world?
Weeder's Digest

What's yellow and round, and 5 miles in circumference?
The Great Ball of China

What's the wedding cake crying for?
It can't stop shedding tiers.

What's a comedian's favorite motorcycle?
A Yamaha-ha

What's got six feet and can't move?
  Two yards

What's a Grecian urn?
  About 500 drachmas a week

What's got long hair and weighs around 2 tons?
  A hippie-potamus

What's wet and says "How do you do" sixteen times?
  Two octopuses shaking hands

What's covered in mud and runs back and forth across the street?
  A dirty double-crosser

What's the time when you've a toothache?
  Tooth-hurty

What's as big as a rhinoceros and weighs nothing?
  A rhinoceros's shadow

What's a skeleton that sleeps all day called?
  Lazy bones

What's musical and steals?
  A robber breaking into song

What's an elastic-band thief called?
  A rubber bandit

What's a fatherless Rice Crispy?
  Snap, crackle—no pop

What's the best way to make a radio?
  Put three wires on a table; take one away—you've got a wireless.

What's a fjord?
  A Scandinavian car

What keeps sheep warm in winter?
  Central bleating

What happened when the Scotsman washed his kilt?
  He couldn't do a fling with it.

Danger! Cannibals, ghosts, and witches

What's a cannibal's favorite breakfast?
Baked beings on toast

What's a cannibal's favorite game?
Swallow my leader

What did the cannibal say to the missionary?
"Dr. Livingstone, I consume."

What does a cannibal's wife make for dinner?
   Good soup—if she's cooked properly

What do cannibals eat at parties?
   Buttered host

What's a sandwich man?
   A cannibal's bag lunch

What do cannibal women look for in their husbands?
   Not a lot—as long as they're edible

What did the cannibal say when she saw a sleeping missionary?
"Oh look! Breakfast in bed."

What's a contented cannibal?
Someone who's fed up with people

What's the highlight of a cannibal wedding?
Toasting the happy couple

What's Count Dracula's favorite coffee?
De-coffin-ated

What do you get if you cross Dracula with Sir Lancelot?
A bite in shining armor

What's got feathers, wings, and fangs?
  Count Duckula

What's Dracula's car called?
  A mobile blood unit

What do you get if you cross Dracula with snow?
  Frostbite

What do famous vampires get on their birthdays?
  Fangmail

What's a graveyard?
  The dead center of the town

What's hot, meaty, and eaten by ghosts?
  Ghoulash

What did the father ghost say to his son?
  "Don't spook until you're spooken to."

What's pink, oinks, and drinks blood?
  A hampire

What's Count Dracula's New York house called?
  The Vampire State Building

What do you get if you cross a policeman with a ghost?
   An inspecter

What did King Kong say to the Empire State Building?
   "Mommy!"

What's wrapped in paper and lives in bell towers?
   The lunchbag of Notre Dame

What makes vampire families stick together?
   Blood is thicker than water.

What's a vampire's favorite fruit?
  A necktarine

What's a vampire's second favorite fruit?
  A blood orange

What's a vampire's favorite song?
  "Fangs for the Memory"

. . . and his favorite soup?
  Scream of tomato

What do witches have for breakfast?
  Snap, cackle, and pop

What's a cannibal who has eaten his mother's sister?
   An aunt-eater

What's a vampire bath?
   A bat tub

What's a vampire's favorite animal?
   A giraffe

What's invisible and plays soccer?
   A ghoulie

What's spooky and ruled France?
   Charles de Ghoul

What weighed 300 pounds and terrorized Paris?
    The Fat-tum of the Opera

What's a missionary's ambition?
    To give cannibals a taste of Christianity

At cross-purposes

What's a cross between an ambassador and a rug called?
  A diplomat

What do you get if you cross a famous detective with a bubble bath?
  Sherlock Foams

What's a skeleton in a kilt called?
  Bony Prince Charlie

What do you get if you cross a chicken with a cement mixer?

A brick layer

What do you get if you cross bacon with a spaceship?

An unidentified frying object

What do you get if you cross a woodwind instrument with an ancient Briton?

An anglo-saxophone

What do you get if you cross a car with a book . . . ?

An autobiography

36

What do you get if you cross the Atlantic with the Titanic?
About 200 miles off the coast of Newfoundland

What do you get if you cross a camera with a crocodile?
A snapshot

What do you get if you cross a worm with a fur coat?
A caterpillar

What do you get if you cross a chicken with a guitar?
A hen that makes music when you pluck it

What do you get if you cross a screwdriver with a cat . . . ?
A tool kitty

. . . and a spaniel, a poodle, and a rooster?
　A cockerpoodledoo

What do you get if you cross a cow, a sheep, and a baby goat?
　The Milky Baa Kid

What do you get if you cross a cow with an octopus?
　An animal that milks itself

What do you get if you cross a cat with a canary?
　A satisfied cat and a dead canary

What do you get if you cross a chicken with a flashlight?
　A battery hen

What do you get if you cross a jeep with a dog?
　A land rover

What do you get if you cross a donkey with its mother . . . ?
　Ass-ma

. . . or a spaniel with a firefly?
　A dog with night vision

What do you get if you cross an elephant with a mouse?
　Enormous holes in the baseboard

What do you get if you cross an elephant with a canary?
　A very messy cage

What do you get if you cross a plumber with a jeweler?
  A ring around the bathtub

What do you get if you cross a rug with a banana?
  A carpet slipper

What do you get if you cross a monkey with a flower?
  A chimp-pansy

What do you get if you cross a cat with an ambulance man?
  A first-aid kitty

What do you get if you cross a horse with a soccer player?
  A centaur forward

What do you get if you cross a jar of jam with an elephant?
  Sandwiches that don't forget

What do you get if you cross an elephant with a kangaroo?
  Huge holes all over Australia

What do you get if you cross a chicken with a kangaroo?
  Pouched eggs

What do you get if you cross a highway with an elephant?
  Run over

What do you get if you cross a chicken with gunpowder?
  An eggsplosion

What do you get if you cross a Muppet with the mist?
   Kermit the fog

What do you get if you cross a Hovercraft with an elf?
   A cross-channel fairy

What do you get if you cross a tape measure with a steam-roller?
   Flat feet

What do you get if you cross a giraffe with a dog?
   An animal that barks at airplanes

What do you get if you cross a Hawaiian dancer with an Indian brave?
    A hula whoop

What do you get if you cross a bee with a quarter pound of ground beef?
    Humburgers

What do you get if you cross an elephant with a crow?
    Lots of broken telephone poles

What do you get if you cross a river with a boat?
    To the other side

What do you get if you cross a daffodil with a calculator?
    A flower with square roots

What do you get if you cross a hyena with a dumb owl?

An animal that no one likes and that doesn't give a hoot

What do you get if you cross a plum with a tiger?

A purple people-eater

What do you get if you cross a jogger with a beach?

Quicksand

What do you get if you cross an airplane with an apple tart?

Pie in the sky

What do you get if you cross a hamburger with a Scotsman?

A Big Mac

What do you get if you cross a top with a puppet?
  Spinocchio

What do you get if you cross a bulb with a frog?
  A croakus

What do you get if you cross a camel with a rose?
  A flower that never needs watering

What do you get if you cross an invader with a roll?
  Attila the Bun

What do you get if you cross a horse with a skunk?
  Whinny the Pyooh

What do you get if you cross a python with a saxophone?
  A snake in the brass

What's that?

What's white on the outside and acts badly?
   A ham sandwich

What's white on the outside and tells rotten jokes?
   A corny beef sandwich

What lies in the gutter and moans loudly?
   A car with a broken windshield

What would you get if all the cars in the U.S. were red?
  A red carnation

What did the cashier say when he was caught stealing?
  "I thought the change would do me good."

What's black, shiny, and serves drinks?
  A crowbar

What's the best way of making a dead dog float?
  Take a scoop of dead dog and a scoop of ice cream.

What's Denice's brother called?
   De nephew

What's warm, greasy, and romantic?
   Chips that pass in the night

What has two legs, rides a broomstick, goes to the seaside, and won't go in the water?
   A chicken sand-witch

What's a computer's favorite food?
   Silicon chips

"What made the chicken cross the road?"
   "I don't know. What made the chicken cross the road?"
      "I'm not sure, but I suppose he had a fowl reason."

What's an Eskimo cow called?
   An Eski-moo

What's an American cow called?
   A Moo Yorker

What's a vampire's good-night kiss?
   Necking

What's a bad-tempered needlework teacher called?
    A proper sew-and-sew

What's the punishment for bigamy?
    Two mothers-in-law

What's the best way to save water?
    Dilute it.

What's the best way to stop people from writing on subway station walls?
    Make the trains run on time.

What's a guillotine?
    A French chopping center

What's poverty?
    Watching the world go buy

What has feathers and drives on the highway?
    Coq-au-van

What's green, big, and doesn't speak all day?
    The Incredible Sulk

What's famous and lives in bathrooms?
    Someone flushed with success

What has a bowler hat and umbrella, and crawls?
    A British civil serpent

What's a glue-covered aspirin good for?
   A man with a splitting headache

What's plastic, runs on batteries, and counts cattle?
   A cow-culator

What's green and for hire?
   A taxi cabbage

What's green and stuffs cabs?
   A Martian taxidermist

What's green, sour, and cleans teeth?
  A tooth pickle

What's worse than raining cats and dogs?
  Hailing taxis

What's yellow and explodes on your pudding?
  Kamikaze custard

What's cowardly, thin, and full of noodles?
  Chicken soup

What's red and green, and sits in the garden going "tick tock, tick tock"?
    A metrognome

What's the easiest way to make a bandstand?
    Take the chairs away.

What's red, squishy, and says "excuse me"?
    A polite strawberry with hiccups

What's white, runs, and lies under the bed with its tongue hanging out?
    A sneaker

What's a signature?
  A baby swan's autograph

What's a sick duck?
  A malardy

What color is a shout?
  Yell-oh

What has feathers and carries water?
  An aqua-duck

What do sheep look for at the sales?
   Baagains

What's a lazy shoe called?
   A loafer

What has eight eyes, a tongue, and tells tales?
   A sneaker

What's bent, salty, and sings rock songs?
   Elvis Pretzel

What's brown, lumpy, and given to actors and actresses?
   Academy awarts

56

What's yellow, has twenty-four legs, and sings?
  Twelve canaries

What's green, noisy and dangerous?
  A thundering herd of cucumbers

What's a ghost's favorite dinner?
  Spookhetti

What's a ghost's favorite breakfast?
  Dreaded wheat

What's mad and travels to the moon?
  A luny module

What's sweet, sour, dangerous, and travels?
   Take-out kung food

What's brown and travels at 110 miles an hour?
   A fuel-injected potato

What's brown, round, and travels at 1,000 miles an hour?
   An intercontinental ballistic rissole

What goes "Ha ha, aaaagh . . ."?
   Someone killing himself with laughter

What's a volcano?
   A mountain that keeps being sick

58

What makes a Maltese Cross?
  A kick in the stomach

What's an Irishman who keeps bouncing off walls called?
  Rick O'Shea

What's a sleeping prehistoric monster called?
  A dinosnore

What's white and runs through the desert with a bedpan?
  Florence of Arabia

What's pink and grows under your nose?
  Tulips

What's long and green and goes "hith, hith"?
    A snake with a lisp

What's purple and swings through the trees in the jungle?
    Tarzan of the Grapes

What's worse than a giraffe with bad bronchitis?
    A centipede with athlete's foot

What's the best way of preventing diseases caused by biting fleas?
    Don't bite fleas.

What's a small Indian guitar called?
  A baby sitar

What's a bad German fighter pilot called?
  Baron von Wrecked Often

What has two legs and talks behind your back?
  A barber

What has two legs and inspects rabbit holes?
  The burrow surveyor

What's a miser vegetarian's greatest dilemma?
    Free meat

What's a man with no legs called?
    Neil (kneel)

What's a one-legged girl called?
    Eileen (I lean)

What has five fingers and drives a tractor?
    A farm hand

What's a man with a shovel in the head called?
    Doug

What's a cow's favorite holiday resort?
  Moo Zealand

What's right and never wrong?
  An angle

What's an astronaut's favorite meal?
  Launch

What's an archaeologist?
  Someone whose career is in ruins

What's a troupe of fat actors called?
  A broad cast

What's the first thing a ball does when it stops rolling?
　It looks round.

What's brown and digs holes when it's fast asleep?
　A bulldozer

What's blue, worn over a shirt, and bursts into flames easily?
　A blazer

What made the cookie box?
　It saw the rum punch.

What's a biplane?
   The last words a pilot says before he bails out

What happened to the two blood clots who fell in love?
   They loved in vein

What's smashing and comes between morning and after-noon?
   A lunch break

What's hot, greasy, and steals cattle?
   A beef-burglar

What's smelly and hums?
   Beethoven's remains decomposing

What does a 6-feet tall, red-haired, green-shoed butcher weigh?
   Meat

What's brown and white, and runs around the forest crying "Mommy, Mommy"?
   Bambi

What's white, creamy, and always comes back to you?
   A boo-meringue

What has two legs and sits in a bacon slicer?
   A butcher getting behind in his deliveries

What's yellow and brown and dances around toadstools?
   A brownie with jaundice

What's the best day to cook bacon and eggs?
   Fry-day

What was Anne Boleyn's last meal?
   Two cold chops

What's boring and moves from branch to branch carrying a briefcase?
    A bank manager

What's furry and worn by nudists?
    Bear skins

What's a bore?
    Someone with nothing to say who says it

What's the shortest bridge in the world?
    The bridge on your nose

What's green and travels at 120 miles an hour?
    A Chevy Sprout

What's a man who buys and sells bugs called?
  An ant-tick dealer

What's pink and white, sharp, and served before a meal?
  A-per-i-teeth

What's tall, dark, and hamsome?
  A very bad actor

What would you shout if you fell off the Matterhorn?
  "A-a-a-a-a-l-p"

What goes "ABC . . . slurp . . . DEF . . . slurp"?
  A kid eating alphabet soup

What's wet and comes out of the bottle at 100 miles an hour?

An Aston Martini

What's an ant that's written a book called?

The author

What's an army?

The thingy up your sleevy

What's a hippie?

The thingy your leggies hang from

What's the best cure for acid indigestion?
　　Stop drinking acid.

What was Noah's profession?
　　Ark-itect

What're two rows of cabbages called?
　　A two-lane cabbage-way

What happened to the cowardly human cannonball?
　　He got fired

What's brown and squeaks when covered with milk?
  Mice crispies

What's meaty, bony, and stands at an angle?
  A lean chop

What's blue, green, yellow, purple, brown, black, and white, and good on the draw?
  A box of crayons

What's small, blue, and eats cakes?
  A blue dwarf cake-eater

What's the best way to make a cigarette lighter?
   Take out some of the tobacco.

What's green and jumps up and down?
   A lettuce at a disco

What's 3 feet tall and rides on the Paris subway?
   Another Métro-gnome

What's brown and fills policeman's sandwiches?
   Truncheon meat

What's soft, wet, and sings?
  Chamois Davis Junior

What's black, sweet, and makes history lessons interesting?
  Dates

What's white, dropped by birds, and angers drivers?
  A deposit on a new car

What's a spaceman's watch?
  A lunartic

What's a midget novelist called?
  A short story writer

What's a snowflakes' dance called?
  A snowball

What's red, blue, and staggers?
  Stupor Man

What's the only thing to eat on a desert island?
  The sandwiches there (sand which is there—*get it!*)

What's locked up and wears a thermos on his head?
  The Man in the Iron Flask

What's got two legs, makes movies, and jumps over trees?
  John Tree-Vaulter

What's the best way of stopping seasickness?
    Bolt your food down.

What's pink and white, comes out at night, and sings in a high voice?
    Falsetto teeth

What's a twain?
    What a wabbit wides on the wailway

What's Batman doing in the tree?
    Looking for Robin's nest

Animal crackers

What's yellow and succeeds?
  A toothless canary

What's an English wasp's favorite TV station?
  The Bee-Bee C

What's gray, hairy, and makes animals yawn?
  A wild bore

What's a mad blackbird called?
  A raven lunatic

What do you get if you cross an insect and a rabbit?
  Bugs Bunny

What's a bee?
  An insect that stings for its supper

What do bees do with honey?
  Cell it

What do you get if you pour boiling water down a rabbit hole?
  Hot cross bunnies

What did the bees go on strike for?
  Shorter flowers and more honey

What has 100 legs and flies?
  Fifty dead birds

What's left after the lawnmower runs over a bird?
  Shredded tweet

What's smaller than a mite's mouth?
  A mite's teeth

What's gray, has sharp teeth, and holds up socks?
   An alligarter

What lies on the ground 100 feet in the air?
   A dead centipede

What's a cow after she gives birth?
   De-calf-inated

What's white when it goes into the water and brown when it comes out?
   A labrador on a snowy day

What's a cat's favorite newspaper?
   Mews of the World

What's brown, got three humps, and lives in the desert?
  A camel with a knapsack

What's yellow and goes "tick tock, tick tock"?
  A clockwork canary

What's white, fluffy, and floats?
  A cat-emeringue

What do you get if you cross a cow with a camel?
  Lumpy milk shakes

What has five legs and gives milk?
  A three-legged cow and a milk-maid

What has 100 legs and goes in one ear and out the other?
   A centipede in a cornfield

What's a three-humped camel called?
   Humphrey

What's black and white and green and brown?
   A cow with a runny nose in a muddy field

What's yellow and goes "Phut . . . phut . . . phut . . ."?
   An outboard canary

What's spotted and untrustworthy?
  A cheetah

What's black, sits in trees, and is highly dangerous?
  A crow with a machine gun

What goes "Cluck, cluck . . . BANG"?
  A chicken in a minefield

What made the chicken run?
  It saw the fox trot

What's a lazy rooster?
   A cockle-doodle don't

What's green, furry, and turns into a 5-ton truck?
   A caterpillar tractor

What's yellow, sings, and weighs a ton?
   Two half-ton canaries

What's yellow, stands in a river during a storm, and doesn't get wet?
   A duck with an umbrella

What's white with black and red spots?
   A dalmatian with measles

What's yellow and goes "kcauq, kcauq"?
  A duck flying backwards

What's "Quack, quack"?
  Double ducks

What's blue and barks?
  A dog in a plastic bag

What's green and doesn't bark?
  The same dog a month later

What's a stupid donkey?
  An animal that makes an ass of itself

What has four legs, barks, and plays tennis?
  John McEn-rover

What has four legs, barks, and dances?
  Natalia Maka-rover

What do you get if you cross an elephant with a mouse?
  Scared cats

What's good for measuring dogs?
  A barking meter

What's a cat that has just swallowed a duck?
    A duck-filled fatty-puss

What would you call a bad-tempered gorilla with cotton wool in its ears?
    Anything you want; it can't hear you

"*What do you get if you cross a mynah bird with a lion?*"
    "I don't know. What do you get if you cross a mynah bird with a lion?"
        "I don't know either. But if it speaks to you, you'd better listen."

What's brown, has four legs, and a trunk?
    A mouse coming back from vacation

What's a Scots parrot?
  A MacCaw

What's a cow's favorite TV show?
  "Dr. Moo"

What's green and turns red at the flick of a switch?
  A frog in an electric blender

What's white one minute and brown the next?
  A white rat in a microwave

What's brown one minute and white the next?
  A brown rat in a freezer

What's green and makes a loud noise?
  A frog horn

What do frogs wear in summer?
  Open-toad sandals

What's a frog's favorite drink?
  Croaka-Cola

What's green and stands in the corner?
  A naughty frog

What has four legs, flies, and cries a lot?
  A mother flea watching her children going to the dogs

What do you get if you cross a giraffe with a hedgehog?
  A very long toothbrush

What makes a giraffe so arrogant?
  It finds it hard to swallow its pride.

What's a hedgehog's favorite lunch?
  Prickled onions

What's best for a sick horse?
    A visit to the horspital

What's a horse's favorite game?
    Stable tennis

What's best for a kangaroo with appendicitis?
    A hoperation

What's sweet and lives in the jungle?
    A meringue-utang

What's gray and out of bounds?
    An exhausted kangaroo

What has antlers and frightens cats?
  Mickey Moose

What's the fastest-growing animal?
  A kangaroo—it grows in leaps and bounds.

What's black-and-white striped, and lives at the North Pole?
  A lost zebra

What's a kangaroo's favorite year?
  A leap year

What's black-and-white, gives milk, and cuts grass?
  A lawn moo-er

What's a louse's favorite party?
    A louse-warming party

"What's green, has ten legs and huge teeth?"
    "I don't know. What's green, has ten legs and huge teeth?"
        "I don't know either. But whatever it is, it's crawling up your back!"

What's brown, whiskered, and cuts grass?
    A lawn miower

What do mice do all day?
    Mousework

What's a mouse's favorite game?
    Hide and squeak

What has four legs and eats off the floor?
   A horse with bad stable manners

What's brightly colored and goes "Hmmmmmmm-choo, hmmmmmmm-choo"?
   A hummingbird with a bad cold

What's covered in feathers and cracks jokes?
   A comedi-hen

What's green and prickly?
   A seasick hedgehog

What has a head, a tail, four legs, and sees equally well in either direction?
A blind horse

What's slithery and good at counting?
An adder

What does a skunk do when it's angry?
It raises a stink.

What did one skunk say to another skunk?
"Let us spray"

What's a termite's favorite breakfast?
  Oak meal

What do frogs fly flags from?
  Tadpoles

What's gray and full of ducks?
  Madame Tussaud's Quacks Works

What's gray, buzzes, and eats cheese?
  A mouse-quito

What's a cat's favorite TV show?
  "Mews at Ten"

What's gray, got twelve legs, and can't see?
  Three blind mice

What's gray, weighs 200 pounds, and says "Here, kitty, kitty"?
  A 200-pound mouse

What's Miss Piggy's favorite perfume?
  Vinegar and honey. (Kermit likes sweet-and-sour pork)

What's gray, squeaks, and ruled Rome?
  Julius Cheeser

What's furry, stings, collects nectar, and is difficult to hear?
    A mumble bee

What's black-and-white and spins round at 60 miles an hour?
    A penguin in a cement mixer

What's made of straw and full of milk bottles?
    A cow's nest

What do you call a 3,000-pound orang-utan?
    "Sir!"

What did the octopus give his wife for Christmas?
    Four pairs of gloves

What makes an octopus a good fighter?
    He's very well armed.

What's creamy and good for sick pigs?
    Oinkment

What do pandas take on holiday?
    The bear essentials

What's pink and writes to pigs?
    A pig's pen pal

What're two hedgehogs called?
    A prickly pair

What's a two-week-old, black-and-white, Russian dog called?

A puppy

What's furry, has whiskers, and chases outlaws?

A posse cat

What's black-and-white and makes a horrible noise?

A penguin playing the bagpipes

What's feathered and sings "Pieces of four! Pieces of four!"?

Short John Silver's parrot

What do porcupines say when they're kissing?
  "Ouch!"

What's black, barks, and runs in the gutter?
  A puddle after it's been raining cats and dogs

What has two legs, a big beak, and hops?
  A pelicangaroo

What good's reindeer?
  "It makes the grass grow—sweetie!"

What's the best way to catch a squirrel?
    Climb a tree and act like a nut.

What has four legs, flies, and tells tales?
    A stool pigeon

What's pink and can't stand still?
    A pig in a tumble drier

What's wooden, howls, and is dangerous?
    A timber wolf

What's green, spicy, and pecks trees?
  Woody Wood Pickle

What's a woodpecker with no beak?
  A headbanger

What's got four legs, barks, and goes "tick tock"?
  A watch dog

What's the worm army called?
  The apple corps

What's black-and-white and runs on sixteen wheels?
   A zebra on roller skates

What's black and red and runs on sixteen wheels?
   A sunburned zebra on roller-skates

What do you get if you cross a zebra with a pig?
   Striped sausages

What do you get if you cross a centipede with a mynah bird?
   A walkie-talkie

What has feathers, flies, and can lift elephants?
    A crane

What's the best way to talk to a man-eating tiger?
    By long-distance telephone

What's extinct and works in rodeos?
    A bronco-saurus

What's 50 feet long and jumps every two seconds?
    A dinosaur with hiccups

What would you get if you crossed a dinosaur with a witch?
A *Tyrannosaurus hex*

What's got feathers and goes "C-c-c-c-c-c-c-c-c-c-c-c-c-c- . . ."?
A rooster with a bad stutter

What's the best way to catch a rabbit?
Hide in a bush and make a noise like a lettuce.

What's a sheep's hairdresser called?
A baa-baa shop

What's a pig's favorite ballet?
Swine Lake

What's hairy, barks, and flies?
  A Skye terrier

What's a myth?
  An unmarried female moth

What has six legs, bites, and talks in code?
  A Morse-quito

What makes Donald Duck fall over?
  Disney spells

What's red and green and jumps out of airplanes?
  A parrot-trooper

What's gray, squeaks, and hangs around in caves?
  Stalagmice

What's suntanned, quacks, and runs his country single-handed?
  A South American duck-tator

What's a spider that has just got married?
  A newly-web

What's brown, quacks, and is full of words?
  A duck-tionary

What's gray, heavy, and sends people to sleep?
  A hypnopotamus

What's brown, has four legs and a yellow beak, and barks?
  A duckshund

What's brown, quacks, and robs safes?
  A safe quacker

What's furry, meows, and chases mice underwater?
  A catfish

What has twelve legs, six ears, and one eye?
  Three blind mice and half a goldfish

What's white and turns cartwheels?
  A white horse pulling a cart

What purrs along the highway and leaves holes in the lawn?
   A Moles Royce

What's a wombat for?
   Playing wom

What's a bald koala bear called?
   Fred Bare

Plummeting the depths

What's brown and yellow and flies along the bottom of the sea?
   A bee in a submarine

What's long, lives underwater, and likes Latin American music?
   A conga eel

What fish never swims?
   A dead one

What fish do shoemakers use everyday?
  Soles and eels

What's battery-powered and good for deaf fish?
  A herring aid

What's brown, lives underwater, and sleeps all day?
  Jack the Kipper

What's got sharp teeth, chops down cherry trees, and never tells lies?
  Jaws Washington

What's 10 yards long, lives in Scotland, and never wins anything?
   The Luck Less Monster

What's yellow and never talks to anyone?
   A lemon sole

What do you get if you cross a sardine with a saber?
   A swordfish

What's the most famous fish?
   The starfish

What lives underwater, has tentacles, and is quick on the draw?
    Billy the Squid

What has tentacles and dances on television?
    The Squids from "Fame"

What's blue, has sharp teeth, and sings?
    Boy Jaws

What made the sand wet?
    The sea wee'ed.

What's silvery, swims in shoals, and goes "Dot, dash, dot, dot"?
    Morse cod

What's black and comes out of the North Sea swearing?
    Crude oil

What's black and comes out of the North Sea saying "Pardon me"?
    Refined oil

What's gray and wears a crown?
    The Prince of Whales

What's pink, lives on the seabed, and is highly dangerous?
   Al Caprawn

What's three years old, has tentacles, and wants to live on land?
   A crazy mixed-up squid

What's blue and chewed by whales?
   Blubber gum

What's a baby whale called?
   A little blubber

What sits on the seabed and shakes?
   A nervous wreck

What's the best way to talk to a fish?
   Drop it a line

What sits at the bottom of the sea and makes you an offer you can't refuse?
   The Cod Father

What's shiny and roars along the seabed at 100 miles an hour?
   A motorpike

Vive la différence

What's the difference between a boxer and a man with a cold?

One knows his blows: the other blows his nose.

What's the difference between a bus driver and a cold?

One knows the stops: the other stops the nose.

What's the difference between a train and a tree?

One leaves its shed: the other sheds its leaves.

What's the difference between a telephone pole and Joan of Arc?

One is made of wood: the other is Maid of Orleans.

What's the difference between a well-dressed man and a tired dog?

The man wears a suit: the dog just pants.

What's the difference between an umbrella and a chatter-box?

You can shut an umbrella up.

What's the difference between a coyote and a flea?

One howls on the prairie: the other prowls on the hairy.

"What's the difference between a donut and a cow?"

"I don't know. What is the difference?"

"Have you ever tried dunking a cow in your coffee?"

What's the difference between a blind man and a sailor in jail?

One can't see to go: the other can't go to sea.

What's the difference between a dog and a flea?

A dog can have fleas: have you ever heard of a flea having dogs?

What's the difference between a man bitten by a mosquito and a man going on vacation?

One is going to itch: the other is itching to go.

"What's the difference between an elephant and a mailbox?"

"I don't know. What's the difference?"

"Remind me never to ask you to mail a letter for me."

What's the difference between a photocopying machine and a flu epidemic?

One makes facsimilies: the other makes sick families.

What's the difference between a married man and a bachelor?

One kisses his Mrs.: the other misses his kisses.

What's the difference between a vegetable gardener and an actor?

One minds his peas: the other minds his cues.

What's the difference between a hairy dog and a painter?
  One sheds his coat: the other coats his shed.

What's the difference between someone going up a staircase
and someone *looking* up a staircase?
  One steps up the stairs: the other stares up the steps.

"*What's the difference between a pitchfork and a tooth-pick?*"
  "I don't know. What is the difference between a pitchfork and a toothpick?"
    "Well if you don't take that pitchfork out of your mouth, you'll hurt yourself."

What's the difference between love and marriage?
  Marriage is forever.

What's the difference between the law and an ice cube?
   Nothing. They're both just-ice!

What's the difference between a seamstress and a nurse?
   One cuts dresses: the other dresses cuts.

What's the difference between a burglar and a man with a wig?
   One has false keys: the other has false locks.

What's the difference between a ball and a prince?
   One is thrown in the air: the other is heir to the throne.

What's the difference between 16 ounces and a pianist?
   One weighs a pound: the other pounds away.

What's the difference between the Prince of Wales and a mother gorilla?
   One is the heir apparent: the other is a hairy parent.

What's the difference between a beer can and a silly Dutchman?
   One is a hollow cylinder: the other is a silly Hollander.

What's the difference between a destroyer and a cheat?
   One rules the waves: the other waives the rules.

What's the difference between a squeeze and a louse?
    One is a bear hug: the other is a hair bug.

What's the difference between a healthy rabbit and an odd person?
    One is a fit bunny: the other is a bit funny.

What's that again?

What's alcoholic and heavy?
  A gin and cement

What's yellow and stupid?
  Thick custard

What's cold and comes in cans?
  Chili beans

What happened when the cat swallowed a ball of wool?
   She had mittens

What's dishonest and coated in cement?
   A hardened criminal

What's the best way to keep Britain clean?
   Send all their rubbish to France

What's found in some cups and can never get out?
   A crack

"What's green, round, grows in fields, and has four wheels?"

"I don't know. What is green, round, grows in fields, and has four wheels?"

"A cabbage. I lied about the wheels."

What's round, has teeth, and bites?
A vicious circle

What stopped the sailors playing cards?
The captain stood on the deck.

What's Camelot known for?
Its good knight life

What's white on the outside and scares easily?
  A chicken sandwich

What's served in glasses and difficult to swallow?
  A stiff drink

What's the laziest letter in the alphabet?
  E, because it's always in bed

What makes young Egyptians good children?
  They hold their mummies in deep respect.

What does an elf do after school?
  Gnome work

What's black, shriveled, and hangs from the ceiling?
  A careless electrician

What's a chicken's favorite cake?
  A layer cake

What's the best thing to do if your cat swallows a dictionary?
  Take the words right out of its mouth.

What makes cooks cruel?
    They beat eggs and batter fish

What's a karate expert's favorite meal?
    Chops

What makes a doctor angry?
    Running out of patients

What's painful and makes holes in the ground?
    A rheumatic drill

What's a doctor who melts in the sun called?
    A plastic surgeon

What do twins speak in Holland?
Double Dutch

What has two legs and goes "put, put, put, put, put, put"?
A very bad golfer

What's the best way to stop children from jumping up and down in bed?
Put Crazy Glue on the ceiling

What's gegs?
Scrambled eggs

What's Mr. and Mrs. Fortune's daughter called?
  Miss Fortune

What swims and gives milk?
  A milk float

What's a miser's first reaction when his house catches fire?
  To pray for rain

What's the fastest drink?
  Milk: it's pasteurized before you see it.

What's always flying and never goes anywhere?
  A flag

What's the hottest show on television?
  "Flame"

What's white on the outside, green in the middle, and jumps?
  A frog sandwich

What's the best way to get rid of excess fat?
  Divorce him.

What's made of wood, sails, and grants wishes?
  A ferry godmother

What has twenty-two legs and goes "crunch, crunch, crunch"?
A soccer team eating potato chips

What's the best butter in the world?
A goat

What's the most slippery country in the world?
Greece

What's pink and wrinkly and belongs to Grandma?
Grandpa

What makes grass so dangerous?
All those blades

What's a cheerful flea called?
  A hoptimist

What has six legs, four eyes, and a tail?
  A horse and rider

What's round, white, and lifts weights?
  An extrastrength aspirin

What stays hot in the fridge?
  Mustard

What's got 500 legs and can't walk?
  Half a millipede

What happened when the fish fought the chips?
   The fish got battered.

What do frogs sit on?
   Toadstools

What exams do farmers take?
   S. Hay T.'s

What's a fisherman paid?
   The net profits

What's alive when it's fed and dead when it's watered?
   A fire

What do you get if you dial 01-493-8939489492-98998989?
 A very sore finger

What's green and sings?
 Elvis Parsley

What's the best way to make an egg roll?
 Push it downhill.

What did the Six Million Dollar Man do when he lost at cards?
 He threw his hand in.

What did the Spanish farmer say to his chickens?
 "Olé!"

What's a 2-foot high comedian?
    A half wit

What's a Hindu?
    Lay eggs

What gets larger the more you subtract?
    A hole

What comes out of the washing machine at 100°F?
    Hot pants

What has four wheels and is full of rabbits?
    A hutch-back car

What's yellow, runny, and shocking?
   Electric honey

What's 6 feet tall, weighs 200 pounds, and can hold up planes?
   A hijacker

What's smelly and comes out firing guns?
   A septic tank

What's small, brown, and carries a suitcase?
   A handle

What has two legs and lives in a cement mixer?
    A hard man

What's good on land, good at sea, and sucks up dirt?
    A Hoovercraft

What color are hiccups?
    Burple

What's round and covered with fingerprints?
    A felt hat

What's the best thing to do if you lose your head?
    Call for a headhunter.

What's Roman and climbs walls?
    IV

What made the jelly wobble?
    It saw the milk shake.

What sits on a shelf and wobbles?
    Jellyvision

What's tall, green, and very wrinkled?
    The Incredible Hulk's granny

What's sweet and musical?
  I-sing sugar

What's a man with a car on his head called?
  Jack

What's a sick joke?
  Something that shouldn't be brought up in conversation

What's sweet and wobbles through the air?
  A jelly-copter

What sits in a stroller and wobbles?
  A jelly baby

What's bald and wobbles?
  Jelly Savalas

What makes Lucy Lucky?
  K

What's hot and goes "hoot, hoot"?
  Kentucky Fried Owl

What happened when the karate champion joined the army?
  He saluted an officer and killed himself.

What's good for water on the knee?
   A tap on the ankle

What's a neurotic young goat called?
   A crazy mixed-up kid

What's big, hairy, and flies at the speed of sound?
   King Concorde

What's a bald detective with a camera called?
   A Kojak instamatic

What's a hungry mathematician's favorite food?
    Anything, as long as it's a square meal

What's Kojak's favorite washing powder?
    Bald

What part of Britain has the stupidest people?
    London—that's where the population is the densest

What's close to silver and cheeky?
    The Lone Ranger's bottom

What's the best thing to do if you find a lion under your bed?
   Sleep somewhere else.

What's short, scared of wolves, and swears a lot?
   Little Red Riding Rude

What's small, irritating, and used after a bath?
   A little thing that's sent to dry us

What's masked and lends money?
   The lone arranger

What happened to the boy with the photographic memory?
   Nothing! It didn't develop.

What's open when it's shut and shut when it's open?
   A drawbridge

What has two heads, one tail, with four legs on one side and two on the other?
   A horse being ridden sidesaddle

What's yellow and deadly?
   Chop-sueycide

What's full of holes and holds water?
   A wet sponge

What's a musical insect?
   A humbug

What's green, bent, and indestructible?
   The Six Million Dollar Cucumber

What's good for nervous elephants?
   Trunkquilizers

What's brown, smelly, and sounds like a bell?
   Dung

What's a mischievous egg called?
   A practical yolker

What's wet and goes upward?
  A backward raindrop

What has feathers and stands in the middle of the road?
  A Rhode Island Red

What's the best way to stop a rooster from crowing on Monday?
  Eat it on Sunday.

What's a spider doing in a bowl of alphabet soup?
  Learning to read

What's a fly doing in a bowl of alphabet soup?
  The breast stroke

What's the bluebottle doing in a bowl of alphabet soup?
  Drowning!

What's after the Stone Age and the Bronze Age?
  The Saus-Age

What's the quickest way to the train station?
  Run as fast as you can.

What's a rude ram?
  Very non-ewe

What's white and goes "baa-baa" splat?
  A sheep falling off a cliff

What has two legs, one wheel, and smells?
    A wheelbarrowful of manure

What's got seven letters and is always spelt wrongly?
    "Wrongly!"

Loony fruit and veg

What's red and green and wears boxing gloves?
  A fruit punch

What's yellow and flashes?
  A banana with a loose connection

What's yellow and always points north?
  A magnetic banana

What's brown, crazy and lives in South America?
   A Brazil nut

What's green on the outside and yellow inside?
   A banana disguised as a cucumber

What's yellow, strong, and very expensive?
   A bunch of bionic bananas

What's yellow and square?
   A banana in disguise

What's purple and frightens people?
  Frankengrape

What's green, hairy, and takes aspirin?
  A gooseberry with a hangover

What's purple and 8,000 miles long?
  The Grape Wall of China

What's purple and conquered the world?
  Alexander the Grape

What's purple and close to France?
  Grape Britain

What's purple and crackles?
  A grape that's not wired up properly

What's purple and glows in the dark?
  A 200-watt grape

What's purple and divides U.S.A. and Canada?
  The Grape Lakes

What's a goose's favorite fruit?
   Gooseberries, of course!

What's green, hairy, and drinks out of the wrong side of the cup?
   A gooseberry with hiccups

What's yellow and 500 yards high?
   The Empire State Banana

What's yellow and wears a mask?
   The Lone Banana

What's yellow and goes "click, click, slip"?
  A ball-point banana

What do you get if you cross a banana with a skunk?
  A skunk with a yellow streak down its back

What did the banana do when the chimpanzee chased it?
  The banana split

What do you get if you cross a banana with a comedian?
  Peels of laughter

What's green and dangerous?
   Angry apples

What's green and goes "bang, bang, bang, bang"?
   A four-door apple

What's the best time to pick apples?
   When the farmer is in bed

What do you get if you cross an apple with an alligator?
   An apple that bites you before you can bite it

What do you get if you cross an apple with a shellfish?
  A crab apple

What's yellow and good at math?
  A banana with a calculator

What's yellow, washable, and doesn't need ironing?
  A drip-dry banana

*What's yellow and goes "beep, beep, b..e e....
ee....e..."?*
  A lemon with a broken horn

What's yellow and goes round and round and round?
  A long-playing lemon

What's red and goes up and down, up and down, up and down, up and down?
    A tomato in a an elevator

What's red, full of seeds, and looks like half a tomato?
    The other half of a tomato

What's green and weighs 20 pounds?
    A plumpkin

What's purple and orbits the Sun?
    The Planet of the Grapes

What's rhubarb?
    Celery that's boiling mad

What would you get if you crossed a lemon with a dino-saur?
   A dino-sour

What's yellow and sweet and holds baby monkeys?
   An ape-ri-cot

What's an apple that is small and yellow at picking time?
   A failure

What's yellow, sour, and goes "splutter, splutter, splutter"?
   A lemon running out of juice

What's brown, hairy, and croaks?
   A coconut with a cold

What's purple and ruled Russia?
  Catherine the Grape

What's purple and burns?
  The Grape Fire of London

What did the chicken say when it found a lemon in the nest?
  "Look at the lemon-mama-laid." (Lemon marmalade)

What's worse than finding a maggot in your apple?
  Finding half a maggot in your apple!

What's furry, whiskered, and sucks lemons?
  A sourpuss

What hangs on a tree and shouts "Help!"?
  A damson in distress

What did the grape say when the elephant trod on it?
  Nothing. It just gave out a little whine.

What did the elephant say to the lemon?
  "Let's play squash."

Oh no! Not another elephant joke

What did the river say when the elephant sat in it?
  "Well, I'll be damned."

What's gray, has a trunk, and takes off from the airport?
  A jumbo jet

What time is it when an elephant sits on your car?
  Time to get a new car

What stopped the two elephants from going for a swim on a hot day?

They only had one pair of trunks between them.

What's best for a blue elephant?

A trip to the circus to cheer him up

What's got four legs and flies?

An elephant that's been dead for a month

What's bright blue and weighs 4 tons?

An elephant holding its breath

What do elephants use to talk to each other?

'elephones

What made the elephant leave the circus?
  It was fed up with working for peanuts.

What's gray, weighs 4 tons, and lives in California?
  An L.A. phant

What weighs 4 tons, has a trunk, and is bright red?
  An embarrassed elephant

What's gray, weighs 4 tons, and wears glass slippers?
  Cinderelephant

What's 2 feet long, has thirty-two eyes, and two tongues?
  An elephant's sneakers

What's gray, weighs 4 tons, and goes "clump, clump, swish, swish"?
An elephant with flippers on its back feet

What's gray, weighs 4 tons, and plays squash?
An elephant in a phone booth

What's gray, weighs 4 tons, and flies?
An elephant in a helicopter

What was the elephant doing on the interstate?
About 10 miles an hour

What animals took longest to get to the Ark?
　The elephants—they had to pack their trunks.

What's an elephant in a fridge called?
　A very tight squeeze

What's yellow, weighs 4 tons, and has a clogged trunk?
　An elephant drowning in a bowl of custard

What's got four ears, eight legs, two tails, four eyes, and two trunks?
　An elephant with spare parts

What's the best way to get five elephants in a subcompact?

Two in the front, two in the back, and one in the glove compartment

What's the best way to get twenty elephants in a subcompact?

Cremate them and put the ashes in the ashtray.

What's red, weighs 4 tons, and sits in a cherry tree?

An elephant disguised as a cherry

What did the elephant say to her naughty child?

"Tusk! Tusk!"

What's feathered and crossed the Alps on elephants?
    Hannibal's army

What did the peanut say to the elephant?
    Nothing. Peanuts can't talk.

What's gray, weighs 4 tons, and leaves footprints in the butter?
    An elephant in the fridge

What do you give a seasick elephant?
    Plenty of room

What's pink, slimy, and weighs 4 tons?
   An inside-out elephant

What's the best thing to do if an elephant charges?
   Pay and run

What's gray and makes you touch the ceiling?
   An elephant under your bed

What's white on the outside, gray in the middle, and heavy in your stomach?
   An elephant sandwich

What do elephants say when they bump into each other?
   "Small world, isn't it?"

What's a hitch-hiking elephant called?
  Stranded

What's gray, weighs 4 tons, and jumps higher than a house?
  An elephant! Houses can't jump.

What's gray, heavy, and sings jazz?
  Elephants Gerald

Vive la différence one more time

What's the difference between an Indian elephant and an African elephant?
   About 3,000 miles

What's the difference between an elephant and spaghetti?
   Elephants don't slip off the end of your fork.

What's the difference between a garden sprinkler and a washerwoman?
   One keeps the lawn wet: the other keeps the laun-dry.

What's the difference between a greedy person and a grill?
    One takes most: the other makes toast.

What's the difference between a monkey and an idiot?
    You can hold a conversation with a monkey.

What's the difference between a small witch and a deer?
    One is a stunted hag: the other is a hunted stag.

What's the difference between a train and a teacher?
    One goes "choo-choo": the other says "Take that gum out of your mouth."

What's the difference between stork and butter?
    Butter can't stand on one leg.

What's the difference between an angry audience and a cow with a sore throat?

One boos madly: the other moos badly.

What's the difference between a dinosaur and a sandwich?

A sandwich doesn't weigh 5 tons.

"What's the difference between a dinosaur and a snew?"

"What's snew?"

"Not a lot. What's new with you?"

What's the difference between a fisherman and a naughty fourth grader?

One baits his hooks: the other hates his books.

What's the difference between a unicorn and a large lettuce?
   One is a funny beast: the other is a bunny feast.

What's the difference between an exhausted hiker and an excited man on the telephone?
   One is a tired walker: the other is a wired talker.

What's the difference between a man who makes $20 bills and a glutton?
   One is a good forger: the other is a food gorger.

What's the difference between a fidget and a bankrupt?
   One can't settle down: the other can't settle up.

What's the difference between a super policeman and a traffic light?

One is a star copper: the other is a car stopper.

What's the difference between an iceberg and a clothes brush?

One crushes boats; the other brushes coats.

What's the difference between a schoolboy and a train engineer?

One has a mind to train: the other has a train to mind.

What's the difference between a hungry man and a greedy one?

One longs to eat: the other eats too long.

What's the difference between a thief and church bells?
  One steals from people: the other peals from steeples.

What's the difference between the North Pole and the South Pole?
  That's a question of degrees.

What's the difference between a cloud and a man standing on a thumbtack?
  One pours with rain: the other roars with pain.

"*What's the difference between a $10 bill and a head of lettuce?*"
  "I don't know."
  "You couldn't lend me lettuce, could you?"

What's the difference between a mirror and a gossip?

One speaks without reflection: the other reflects without speaking.

What's the difference between Italian grapes and Scots ones?

The Italian ones have a better suntan

What's the difference between a Boeing 747 and a lemon?

A lemon can't cross the Atlantic without refueling.

What's the difference between a sailor and a bargain hunter?

One sails the seas: the other sees the sales.

"*What's the difference between a pound and the ocean?*"

"I don't know. What's the difference between a pound and the ocean?"

"Weight and sea!"

What's the difference between a newspaper and a TV?
Have you ever tried swatting a fly with a TV?

What's the difference between an oak tree and tight shoes?
One makes acorns: the other makes corns ache.

What's the difference between a jeweler and a jailer?
One sells watches: the other watches cells.

What's the difference between a tailor and a horse trainer?
  One tends mares; the other mends tears.

What's the difference between a composer and a postman?
  One writes notes; the other delivers them.

What's the difference between a young lady and a fresh loaf?
  One is a well-bred maid: the other is well-made bread.

What's the difference between an ice cream and a bully?
  You lick one: the other licks you.

A little eavesdropping

What did Adam say to his wife on December 24th?
  "It's Christmas Eve."

What did the man say when he walked into a bar?
  "Ouch!"

What did the right soccer cleat say to the left soccer cleat?
  "Between us we'll have a ball."

What were Anne Boleyn's last words?
    "I think I'll go for a walk around the block."

What did Cinderella say when her holiday snapshots were late?
    "Someday my prints will come."

What did the cucumber say to the jam jar?
    "If you'd kept your mouth shut, I wouldn't be in this pickle."

What did the cat say when it was run over?
    "I don't have the guts to do anything about it!"

What did the calculator say to the geometry book?
   "Between us we've got a lot of problems."

What did the big chimney say to the little chimney?
   "You're far too young to smoke."

What did the cashier say to the register?
   "I'm counting on you."

What did the chocolate say to the lollipop?
   "Hello, sucker."

What did the cookie say when it was run over?
    "Oh, crumbs!"

What did the macramé expert say to the string?
    "Get knotted."

What did the doctor say to the Invisible Man?
    "Next, please."

What did the mayonnaise say to the fridge?
    "Shut the door. I'm dressing."

What did the flea say to Robinson Crusoe?
  "See you on Friday."

What did the flea say to the other flea?
  "Shall we walk or take the cat?"

What did the big hand say to the little hand?
  "Got a minute?"

What did the little hand say to the big hand?
  "See you on the hour."

What did Hamlet say to the weight watchers?
   "Tubby or not tubby?"

What did the doctor say to the Invisible Man's wife?
   "I can't see anything wrong with your husband."

What does the sea say to the sand?
   Not a lot. It usually waves.

What did the sock say to the shoe?
   "See you soon: I've gotta run."

What did the big toe say to the little toe?
   "Don't look now: we're being followed by a couple of heels."

What did the traffic light say to the car?
   "Don't look while I'm changing."

What did one tonsil say to the other tonsil?
   "It must be spring: here comes a swallow."

What did the tonic water say to the gin?
   "I'm diluted to meet you."

What did the pencil say to the eraser?
    "Take me to your ruler."

What did one ear say to the other ear?
    "Between you and me, we need a haircut."

What did the carrot say to the potato?
    "Stop making eyes at me."

What did the painter say to the wall?
    "One more crack like that and I'll plaster you."

What did the strawberry say to the other strawberry?

"If we hadn't been in bed together, we wouldn't be in this jam."

What did the wall say to the plug?

"Socket to me, baby."

What did one handcuff say to the other handcuff?

"Why don't you join me?"

What did the arthritis say to the rheumatism?

"Let's get out of this joint."

What did the jack say to the car?
  "Wanna lift?"

What did the launch pad say to the rocket?
  "Clear off—you're fired!"

What did the frankfurter say to the ketchup?
  "That's enough of your sauce."

What did the scissors say to the paper?
  Something very cutting.

What did the soil say to the rain?
  "Stop, or my name is mud."

What did the necklace say to the crown?
  "You go on ahead: I'll hang around."

What did the right eye say to the left eye?
  "Between ourselves, there's something that smells."

What did one sheik say to the other sheik?
  "Oil see you again."

What did the puddle say to the rain?
  "Drop in sometime."

What did the digital watch say to the alarm clock?
  "Look, no hands."

What did the mother worm say to the baby worm?
  "You're late. Where on earth have you been?"

What did the petroleum sing to the coal?
  "What kind of fuel am I?"

What did the squirrel say to his girlfriend?
  "I'm nuts about you!"

What did the raindrop say to the others?
  "Two's company: three's a cloud."

What did the appendix say to the kidney?
  "The doctor's taking me out tonight."

What did the bee say to the rose?
  "Hi bud."

What did the rose say to the bee?
   "Buzz off."

What did the brush say to the vacuum cleaner?
   "Heard the latest dirt?"

What did the queen bee say to the naughty drone?
   "Behive yourself."

What did Little John say when Robin Hood fired at him by mistake?
   "That was an arrow escape."

What did the alarm clock say to the rain?
   "Stop. I'm ringing wet."

What did the wood say to the drill?
   "Go away. You bore me."

What did the window say to the venetian blind?
   "If it wasn't for you it'd be curtains for me."

What did the girl watch say to the boy watch?
   "Keep your hands to yourself."

What did the pool ball say to the other pool ball?
  "Don't move until you get your cue."

What did the doctor say to the pale orange?
  "You look off-color; are you peeling well?"

What did the religious carrot say to the greens?
  "Lettuce pray."

The Irish never speak well of one another

(Dr. Johnson)
So why should we? (Ed.)

What's dead and climbs walls?
  An Irish ghost

What's found in Dublin and called "Spot"?
  An Irishman's pet zebra

What happened when the Irishman changed his mind?
  His new one didn't work either.

What happened when the Irishman tried to blow up a bus?
    He burned his mouth on the exhaust pipe.

What takes off in New York and lands in Paris?
    An Aer Lingus flight to Dublin

What happened to the Irish sea scout?
    His tent sank.

What happened to the Irish tap dancer?
    He broke his leg when he fell in the sink.

What happened to the Irishman when he put some toilet water on after shaving?

He was knocked out when the lavatory seat fell on his head.

What's small, crawls, and chews bricks?

An Irish woodworm

What sits at a piano spinning round and round?

An Irishman trying to play the piano stool

What goes into shops and puts things back on the shelves?

An Irish kleptomaniac

What do you get if you cross a monkey with an Irishman?
  A stupid monkey

What made the Irishman cross the road?
  He wanted to get to the middle.

What's 5 yards long with an IQ of 50?
  Fifty Irishmen in a bus line

What's green and served hot, straight from the oven?
  An Irish salad

What's got four letters and is found at the top and bottom of an Irish stepladder?
  "Stop"

What's 10 feet tall and lives in Dublin?
  Paddy Long Legs

What did the Irish spy do when he found his room was bugged?
  Sprayed it with DDT

What happened to the Irish glass-blower?
  He inhaled and got a pane in his stomach.

What's white and runs backwards in slow motion?
  The Six Million Dollar Irishman

At cross-purposes again

What do you get if you cross a chicken with a banjo?
A self-plucking chicken

What do you get if you cross a magician with a helicopter?
A flying sorcerer

What do you get if you cross a hyena with a bouillon cube?
An animal that makes a laughing stock of itself

What do you get if you cross a rabbit with a spider?
   A harenet

What do you get if you cross a cowboy with a stew?
   Hopalong Casserole

What do you get if you cross a baby, a soldier and an electric bulb?
   A member of the light infant-ry

What do you get if you cross an iceberg with an alligator . . . ?
   A cold snap

. . . and an iceberg with a witch?
  A cold spell

What do you get if you cross a germ with a comedian?
  Sick jokes

What do you get if you cross a grade school with Sir Lancelot?
  A knight school

What do you get if you cross a hyena with a mynah bird?
  An animal that laughs at its own jokes

What do you get if you cross a stream and a river?
    Wet feet

What do you get if you cross an old Egyptian with a door bell?
    Toot-en-come-in

What do you get if you cross a flat fish with George Washington?
    The flounder of the U.S.A.

What do you get if you cross Dracula with a dwarf?
    A vampire that bites kneecaps

What do you get if you cross a microphone with a dressing gown?

A mike-robe

What do you get if you cross Dan Rather with a potato?

A common-tator!

What do you get if you cross a mynah bird with a homing pigeon?

A bird that can ask its way home if it gets lost

What do you get if you cross an encyclopedia with a pair of trousers?

Smarty pants

What would you get if you crossed a watchdog with a werewolf?

Very nervous postmen

What do you get if you cross an angry comic with rolls straight from the oven?

Hot cross puns

What do you get if you cross a pig with a naked runner?

Streaky bacon

What do you get if you cross a policeman with Oprah Winfrey?

An arresting personality

What do you get if you cross a porcupine with a mole?
  Tunnels that leak

What do you get if you cross a pop singer with a seat?
  A rocking chair

What do you get if you cross a railway engine with chewing gum?
  A chew-chew train

What do you get if you cross a thief with an orchestra?
  Robbery with violins

What do you get if you cross a skunk with an eagle?
  An animal that stinks to high heaven

What do you get if you cross a pig with a highway?
  A road hog

What would you get if you crossed an elephant with a rooster?
  An animal that wakes people who live on the top floor

What do you get if you cross an elephant with a rubber band?
  An animal that never forgets snap decisions

What would you get if you crossed an elephant with a computer?

A big know-it-all

What would you get if you crossed an elephant with a skunk?

A big stinker

What do you get if you cross a racehorse with a giraffe?

An animal that's difficult to ride but great in a photo finish

What do you get if you cross a cow with an Arab?

A milk sheik

What do you get if you cross a chicken with an electric organ?

Hammond eggs

What do you get if you cross an elephant with the abominable snowman?

A jumbo Yeti